A season that will go down in history

What was your moment this season? The win over Chelsea at Stamford Bridge? The one that followed, at home to the might of Manchester United?

Perhaps the 4-3 triumph at West Ham in the Boleyn Ground's final season, thanks to Callum Wilson's maiden Premier League hat-trick, gets your vote?

Or maybe it was the stunning 2-0 win at home, under the Vitality Stadium lights, against south coast neighbours Southampton that lit up this most memorable of seasons?

Regardless of those individual memories, for most AFC Bournemouth fans, this will always be 'the season'. The club's first in the Premier League.

For those of the older generation, the supporters who had previously put in the hard miles to places like Rochdale, Bury, Hartlepool and Carlisle, often to watch defeats, this season will always be the reward for their years of solid and unwavering support.

But this season has also welcomed a new generation of Cherries supporters, those enthralled by the way Eddie Howe's side play the game, their spirit and work-rate.

While Leicester's title win has taken the late-season plaudits and attention, this team's achievement of staying in this most unforgiving of divisions should not be underestimated.

In this publication, I hope we have captured the feelings of the supporters, both in words and pictures, during what will go down in club history as AFC Bournemouth's greatest achievement.

Up the Cherries...

NEIL MELDRUM, editor

The team...

Editor: Neil Meldrum
Words: Neil Perrett, Ned Payne, Andy Mitchell
Design: Neil Meldrum
Pictures: Corin Messer, Sam Sheldon, Richard Crease, Mick Cunningham, Focus Images

Follow Cherries' fortunes online at
bournemouthecho.co.uk/sport

Printed by...

reaction Group

Reaction Group, JPS House, 1 Dalling Road, Branksome, Poole, BH12 1DJ
■ Tel 01202 757579
■ info@reaction-group.co.uk
■ www.reaction-group.co.uk

Contents

Published by Newsquest Media (Southern) Ltd, Richmond Hill, Bournemouth, BH2 6HH

carbrini
AFC BOURNEMOUTH

'From the start of the season to now there has been real growth'

WORDS: **NED PAYNE**

Boss Eddie Howe has picked his three favourite moments from the Premier League campaign after Cherries achieved safety.

Callum Wilson's opener in the 4-3 win at West Ham in August kicked off the list, the striker going on to net a hat-trick as Cherries banked their first victory in the top flight.

Howe also selected Junior Stanislas's dramatic leveller at home to Everton which earned Cherries a 3-3 draw in the eighth minute of second-half stoppage-time.

Completing the list was substitute Glenn Murray's close-range header at Chelsea at the beginning of December, an 82nd-minute effort which secured Cherries a first competitive win at Stamford Bridge.

Asked to reflect on the memorable moments of the season, Howe told the Daily Echo: "The first would be our first goal against West Ham. We hadn't scored or picked up a point and we broke that at West Ham so impressively.

"I thought Callum's goal was a watershed moment for us and then the game exploded in the way it did and we got three crucial points.

"I think the Everton game was a turning point with the last-gasp goal from Junior – that was a big moment in our season.

"Then of course Glenn's winner at Chelsea. That was a different type of performance where we had our backs to the wall for most of the game but that was a huge moment as well."

The majority of Cherries' players had not played in the Premier League before the 2015-16 campaign and many – such as Simon Francis, Marc Pugh and Tommy Elphick – had made the journey with the club from League One.

Howe felt there had been gradual improvement in the squad over the course of the campaign but insisted there could be even more to come.

He added: "From the start of the season to now there has been real growth – maybe in some players more than others – but when you look at the squad as a whole I definitely think we've improved.

"The demands placed upon us were naturally going to bring improvement anyway because you are playing against the very best in the world and the players are being pushed all the time.

"As a team, I think we have naturally become more experienced and we are getting used to the level. But I still think there is more room for improvement.

"I would always look at the table and think we can move up. I believe in the players and what we do.

"I'm never one to look at the table and think anything other than 'we've got to try and win some games'."

'It is our greatest ever achievement. It's an honour to captain this club'

WORDS: **NEIL PERRETT**

Inspirational Cherries skipper Tommy Elphick hailed staying in the Premier League as "by far the greatest achievement in this club's history".

Elphick had already written his name indelibly in the Dean Court record books having led Cherries to promotion from both League One and the Championship.

But the 28-year-old defender surpassed his previous exploits by captaining the Dorset club as they capped a memorable campaign by preserving their top-flight status.

Elphick said: "When you look at the teams we came up against and the financial power of some of them, it was by far the club's greatest achievement.

"We did it in style and overcame some awful setbacks. We had the spine of the team ripped out early in the season and could easily have used that as an excuse.

"But that is not how we operate as players or how the manager and his staff work. You never heard anybody inside the camp moaning about injuries, bad luck or injustices.

"Every setback was seen as a challenge to overcome and that was what spurred us on. We remained grounded through the tough times and the good times.

"I have the utmost respect for every former player and manager of this football club. I know there have been some great times in the past with promotions and cup wins.

"But this was the first season the club had competed at the very top level of the English game and, for that reason, I believe staying in the Premier League is the greatest achievement.

"It is an honour to captain this club and this is something I will look back on with immense pride after I have retired.

"The beauty of the squad and the manager is that we only ever look forward. We are always looking to break new barriers and are already thinking about the next one. It is about laying solid foundations and getting momentum going into next season.

"I would also like to give a special mention to our loyal supporters. I know there have been some tough times at this football club in the not-too-distant past and the fans really stuck with it. We appreciated their support throughout the season and staying in the Premier League is as much for them as it is for us."

Elphick also had words of praise for Simon Francis who donned the captain's armband during his injury absence.

He said: "It wasn't easy for him when I came out of the team because we weren't winning as many games as we would have liked.

"You have to remain calm and be true to yourself. You have to keep working hard to set the example and he did that. He did very well to captain the team through some tough times."

TEAM
NEMOUTH

'Going on runs in the Prem is what makes or breaks your season'

WORDS: **ANDY MITCHELL**

Chelsea, Manchester United, Southampton.

The joy of those Roy of the Rovers-style nights probably still intoxicate Cherries supporters now at the end of this landmark maiden journey into Premier League territory.

Indeed, as many onlookers have pointed out, top-flight status could well have been in greater doubt had points not been pocketed from the big occasions.

But Simon Francis believes the cornerstone of a fruitful campaign is bigger than that, particularly after an October and November that flattened expectation and drained all bar the last few droplets of hope.

So while arresting the slide with a 1-0 victory at Stamford Bridge caught the attention of a worldwide audience, Francis argues battling draws with Swansea and Everton prior to that were just as vital in the context of the club's ultimate goal.

"Before the season started, we watched Premier League games in the same way everybody else does and backed ourselves with a fully-fit squad," said Francis.

"We had to re-analyse where we were going when we had the injuries and survival was our main aim.

"It did have an effect on the lads psychologically. We knew it would be an uphill struggle and even more so with key players getting injured so early on and in the same game.

"The combination of things that happened was a huge blow for us. We had to regroup and realise what we had within the squad and what we had to go out and get.

"It was our target to get to January when the manager could boost the squad, which he did a brilliant job with."

In the end, Cherries did more than merely muddle through.

After toppling the champions and Manchester United, the battling triumph at West Brom and precious point against an in-form Crystal Palace saw Cherries push away from the bottom three.

And with resources boosted during the January transfer window, smaller but no less significant runs followed.

The beating of Norwich was turned into a sequence by claiming a precious point at Sunderland and then a victory at Palace at the start of a February that soon became a month to forget.

But a 0-0 draw at Watford prompted another flurry of three straight victories – against Southampton, Newcastle and Swansea – that all but sealed the deal.

"We picked up the points and going on those runs in the Premier League is what makes or breaks your season," said Francis. "They have been key.

"We had a great sequence where we picked up lots of points, particularly after Christmas when we started to break away from the teams at the bottom.

"Now, the aim is the same as it has always been, to go again, to improve again and to take everything on to the next level."

JD
MANSION
明陞
CAPTAIN
e-X-tech

MANSION

'There are no words to describe how proud I am of every player'

JEFF MOSTYN WRITES EXCLUSIVELY FOR PREMIER DAYS

Short of writing a book, it is going to be difficult to sum up in a few words the incredible achievement of the class of 2015-16, not only in respect of the season but in terms of the club's history.

So many plaudits have been lavished on Eddie Howe and the team from around the globe it would be impossible for any football fan anywhere on the planet to be oblivious to what this team has achieved.

At the start of the season, the bookmakers were unanimous in making us favourites to be relegated, so I would like to start by thanking them for providing the inspiration to prove them wrong.

It is no coincidence that the rags to riches rise of the club has been based, among other things, on a siege mentality.

Despite points deductions and transfer embargoes, under the guidance of Eddie Howe, the club has always defied the odds and succeeded. We now know this season was to be no exception.

Put into context, I believe retaining our position in the Premier League is the greatest achievement in this club's long history and surpasses last year's achievement of winning the Championship.

The Premier League is not recognised as the world's number one league for nothing. It is the most popular, most compelling, most competitive, most-watched league on earth and we remain part of it as a result of the team's extraordinary performances in our inaugural season.

This season's success has not just been about the players. Huge credit should go to Eddie, Jason, all of their support staff and a special mention to our medical and sports science staff who have worked tirelessly to get players back into the team and others on the road to recovery.

There is also a remarkable team running the club that make everything on the pitch possible.

Our owner Maxim Denim, without whom this would not have been possible, our shareholders, chief executive Neill Blak, general manager Liz Finney, Alice Jeans our PA, Neil Vacher our secretary, all of our commercial, design, media, finance, catering, superstore and ticketing teams and, not to forget, our matchday stewards and medical teams.

We are privileged to have such amazing staff at the club. On behalf of my fellow directors and new investors, thank you all.

There is, of course, another group of people who have had a significant influence on the club's success.

Our incredible supporters, home and away, have provided the team with the vocal inspiration that has often influenced matches.

Last, but by no means least, it is time to lavish superlatives on the players. No matter what goes on behind the scenes, the only thing that matters is what happens on the pitch.

Each and every one of our squad has performed at the highest level and there are no words to describe how proud I am of every single player. We have retained our place among the world's elite because of them.

MANSION
30

❶ Matt Ritchie in action on the opening day of the season
❷ Marc Pugh stays in control
❸ Villa celebrate their winner in front of the East Stand

MATCHDAY ONE: CHERRIES 0 ASTON VILLA 1

VITALITY STADIUM

08.08.15

Substitute Rudy Gestede's second-half header took the gloss off Cherries' big day as the club's debut in the Premier League ended in defeat.

Eddie Howe's team were left to rue a combination of wasteful finishing and excellent goalkeeping as they failed to take advantage of their first-half dominance.

Cherries created three good chances in the final nine minutes of the first period with Dan Gosling missing from close range and Villa goalkeeper Brad Guzan making smart saves to deny Callum Wilson and Marc Pugh.

And they were made to pay when Villa's new signing Gestede came off the bench to sucker-punch them with 18 minutes remaining.

Boss Howe said: "I thought we were outstanding in the first half. I was very pleased with the display and all that was missing was goals.

"We got hit with a sucker-punch set-play in the second half and learned what the Premier League is all about and how difficult it is going to be if you aren't clinical.

"But there were plenty of positives and a lot to work on. Some of the football we played in both halves was right out of the top drawer.

"We asked the players to be brave and progressive and I thought they were. They worked incredibly hard and I felt they left it all on the pitch so I can't be disappointed with that. We will look at things and try to get better but I was very pleased overall. I had to be."

JD
JD
MANSION
明陞
Standard Chartered
LFC
24
20
AFC

❶ Lee Tomlin battles with Adam Lallana
❷ Tommy Elphick keeps his eyes on the ball
❸ Cherries look dejected after Christian Benteke's goal
❹ Callum Wilson appeals
❺ Steve Cook in action
❻ Callum Wilson keeps Dejan Lovren at arm's length

MATCHDAY TWO: LIVERPOOL 1 CHERRIES 0

ANFIELD 17.08.15

A controversial goal from Liverpool striker Christian Benteke condemned Cherries to a second successive defeat on their first visit to Anfield in 47 years.

Benteke struck midway through the first half despite Philippe Coutinho appearing to have taken up an offside position moments before the Belgian had tapped home.

It was a bitter pill to swallow for the visitors, who also had an early effort from Tommy Elphick ruled out after the captain had been judged to have fouled Dejan Lovren.

To compound Cherries' frustrations, the Premier League later confirmed referee Craig Pawson had been wrong to allow Benteke's goal to stand as it had contravened new offside laws.

Max Gradel, who had been recruited from St Etienne for a fee of £6million, was given his first start.

Elphick was "100 per cent" certain his effort should have stood and told the Daily Echo: "I felt like I had got a march on Lovren and used my hands to elevate myself, get above him and keep myself there.

"I had my hands above his shoulders and the ref penalised me for pushing. There was nothing in it. I think he felt like he was scrambling a bit and reacted to my hands being on his shoulders but when you go up for a header, you cannot jump with your arms by your side.

"Things happen so quickly and the officials have a difficult job. The goal should have stood but it went against us and we cannot change anything now."

❶ Marc Pugh celebrates his first Premier League goal
❷ Eunan O'Kane and Carl Jenkinson
❸ Callum Wilson on the run
❹ Eddie Howe and Slaven Bilic
❺ Callum Wilson celebrates

MATCHDAY THREE: WEST HAM UTD 3 CHERRIES 4

THE BOLEYN GROUND

22.08.15

Callum Wilson bagged the club's first top-flight hat-trick and Marc Pugh reached a memorable goalscoring milestone as Cherries broke their duck in some style at Upton Park.

Wilson put Cherries 2-0 in front inside 28 minutes before Mark Noble's penalty and Cheikhou Kouyate's 53rd-minute goal restored parity for the Hammers.

Pugh's finely-taken effort midway through the second-half edged Cherries in front and saw the winger join an elite band of players to have scored in the top five divisions of English football.

Wilson's penalty 11 minutes from time saw him leave with the match-ball before Modibo Maiga's strike made for a nervy final eight minutes for Cherries and their followers.

Cherries boss Eddie Howe paid tribute to Pugh when he said: "He epitomises everything we stand for.

"With every challenge he has been given during his time here, he has responded positively, improved and grown, just as the club has.

"I think his attitude off the pitch epitomises everything we stand for and he deserves the accolade of having scored in the top five divisions – you've never met a more dedicated, nice guy."

Wilson said: "Scoring a hat-trick in the Premier League is something you dream of.

"It is the first hat-trick of my career and I think I have been waiting to get to the Premier League to do that."

明陞
MANSION
JD
13
4

DE LAET
2
11
4

15
KING
10
B&H

MANSION
32

❶ Callum Wilson wheels away after his goal
❷ Tyrone Mings goes down under a challenge from Danny Drinkwater and his season is over
❸ Lee Tomlin battles with Robert Huth
❹ Eunan O'Kane on the charge
❺ Eddie Howe and Claudio Ranieri
❻ Matt Ritchie in action
❼ Tommy Elphick awaits the ball

MATCHDAY FOUR: CHERRIES 1 LEICESTER CITY 1

VITALITY STADIUM

29.08.15

Eunan O'Kane held up his hand to admit his mistake had proved costly as Cherries let two points slip after being pegged back late on by the Foxes.

The midfielder squandered possession to N'Golo Kante near the halfway line before Jamie Vardy embarked on a run which ended with him being brought down for a penalty.

And Vardy, who was felled by Steve Cook, salvaged a point for the visitors when he rammed home the spot kick despite the best efforts of Cherries goalkeeper Artur Boruc.

Vardy's 86th-minute penalty was the first goal of a record-breaking run for the Leicester striker and cancelled out Callum Wilson's stunning overhead kick opener.

O'Kane said: "I have to hold up my hand. I should have done better and it was a lesson for me personally. I have learned the hard way."

However, boss Howe leapt to O'Kane's defence when he said: "It works two ways.

"You can't have someone on the ball and have no options ahead.

"We've got some very good technical players and if we concede goals from giving away the ball in tight areas then I will take the blame because that is how I want my players to play. There will be no finger pointing, we just need to do better in general."

Cherries were rocked during the game when both Tyrone Mings and Max Gradel sustained what would prove to be long-term knee injuries.

❶ Joshua King in action
❷ Agony for Cherries as Norwich score
❸ Glenn Murray on the run
❹ Eddie Howe looks dejected
❺ Nathan Redmond celebrates
❻ Steve Cook wins the ball

MATCHDAY FIVE: NORWICH CITY 3 CHERRIES 1

CARROW ROAD

12.09.15

Sporting their new pink away kit for the first time, Cherries left Carrow Road with red faces having been on the receiving end of a heavy beating.

Goals from Cameron Jerome, Wes Hoolahan and Matt Jarvis eased the Canaries into a 3-0 lead, with Cherries fortunate to escape further punishment.

A calamitous 15-minute spell in the second half set the alarm bells ringing as Cherries were sliced open. Hoolahan and Jarvis profited from some charitable defending and it could have been worse had Robbie Brady not hit the woodwork

Although Steve Cook threw them a lifeline with an 81st-minute headed effort, it proved a false dawn as Howe's team left Norfolk with their tails between their legs.

Howe urged on his players when he said: "I think you have to use the pain that you feel from defeat to motivate yourself to come again and to come again stronger.

"That has always been our way. We have had defeats and low spells before. It doesn't change. It is about making sure the group is ready to put those mistakes right.

"I don't think there is any reality check needed. We were always aware how difficult this season was going to be and how big a challenge it would be.

"I had been really pleased with our performances and this was our first disappointing game. I think you are going to have that throughout a season."

VAN AANHOLT

❶ Matt Ritchie lets fly with a goal of the season contender
❷ Callum Wilson celebrates his goal

MATCHDAY SIX: CHERRIES 2 SUNDERLAND 0

VITALITY STADIUM

19.09.15

Matt Ritchie's first-half wonder strike helped Cherries claim their first home victory of the season, while Callum Wilson also scored early on to register his fifth goal in four Premier League games.

Ritchie's spectacular chest-volley gave the home side a two-goal lead inside the first 10 minutes at Vitality Stadium.

Sunderland had a Jeremain Lens header harshly ruled out for offside in the second half before Younes Kaboul picked up his second booking for a foul on Wilson to compound the Black Cats' misery.

While Ritchie admitted his peach had topped his list of best goals, he also insisted modestly: "It's my job."

The Scottish international's stupendous 25-yard volley from a headed clearance created a whirlwind of reaction with pundits lauding it as an early goal-of-the-season contender.

Ritchie said: "It is great to have recognition for the things you do but it is your job.

"That is what you're there for, to try to help your team.

"I am just delighted to play a part in a fantastic team performance and, more importantly, get three points on the board.

"I would say it was my best goal. As soon as it left my foot, I knew I had hit it sweetly so I was delighted to see it hit the top corner.

"I watched it back on Match of the Day and yes, the Sky Plus was on!"

❶ Callum Wilson lies injured
❷ Matt Ritchie and Steve Cook in action
❸ Simon Francis keeps his eyes on the ball
❹ The teams emerge from the tunnel
❺ Eddie Howe in the dugout

MATCHDAY SEVEN: STOKE CITY 2 CHERRIES 1

THE BRITANNIA STADIUM

26.09.15

Defeat at Stoke was overshadowed by the untimely death of popular former Cherries employee and freelance photographer Mick Cunningham, who had been working at the Britannia Stadium on behalf of the Daily Echo sports desk.

Cherries boss Eddie Howe said: "Mick's loss was so sudden and he will be greatly missed. On behalf of everyone at the club, I would like to send our condolences to his family.

"He was a friendly face and a really genuine guy who would show a genuine interest in everybody. He gave everything to our football club. People like that are so important because they make you feel comfortable and appreciated. Mick had an incredible work ethic and dedication to his job. And he always did it with a smile on his face. It is such sad news."

Stoke took the lead in controversial circumstances through Jon Walters after 32 minutes and Mame Biram Diouf bagged the winner seven minutes from time after Dan Gosling had levelled.

Cherries were further rocked when Callum Wilson became the third player to suffer a serious knee injury, the striker falling awkwardly following a challenge by Philipp Wollscheid.

Howe said: "We certainly didn't foresee what happened. In football, you never know what's round the corner. It does make it very difficult for us to recover.

"It's unbelievably bad luck. You wouldn't wish a serious injury on any footballer and to get three in one team, key players as well, is mystifying."

RITCHIE
30
KING
17
ABDI
22

MATCHDAY EIGHT: CHERRIES 1 WATFORD 1

VITALITY STADIUM
03.10.15

Cherries' draw with fellow new boys Watford was a tale of two penalties and a costly blunder from goalkeeper Artur Boruc.

Eddie Howe's team took the lead thanks to Glenn Murray's 28th-minute opener before a Boruc mistake gifted the visitors a route back into the game just before half-time.

The Pole received possession from defender Sylvain Distin and his attempted return pass was cut out by Odion Ighalo, who shimmied past the stopper and slotted home.

To cap a disappointing day, Murray then saw his second-half penalty kept out by the inspired Heurelho Gomes, one of a number of top-drawer saves from the Brazilian, including another to prevent Steve Cook's overhead kick from winning the day for Cherries.

Boss Howe said: "Artur is experienced enough to know and has worked long enough with us to know that there is no hangover from that mistake and that it's business as usual.

"It's back to work to make ourselves better, no matter whether we win, lose or draw.

"It was one of those things. We encourage our players and our goalkeeper to be brave and to take responsibility to play from the back. That is very much our philosophy."

Howe added: "There's no blame attached to Glenn, it's just one of those things. If you are brave enough to take a penalty, there is a chance you could miss it. I thought Glenn was excellent and scored a very good goal."

❶ Matt Ritchie whips in a free kick
❷ Matt Ritchie and Charlie Daniels in action
❸ Andrew Surman gets stuck in
❹ Glenn Murray after his goal

SMITH
15

30

MANSION

STAD
MANSION

❶ Glenn Murray battles with City keeper Joe Hart
❷ Simon Francis in action at the Etihad
❸ Cherries react after a City goal
❹ Glenn Murray rues a missed chance
❺ Dan Gosling tussles with Fernandinho
❻ Murray chases back

MATCHDAY NINE: MANCHESTER CITY 5 CHERRIES 1

ETIHAD STADIUM

17.10.15

Injury-hit Cherries were no match for Manchester City as Raheem Sterling netted the first hat-trick of his career to condemn the visitors to a heavy defeat at the Etihad.

The England man was in clinical mood and took the game away from Cherries by plundering his treble in the first half with Glenn Murray's 22nd-minute goal proving a false dawn.

Wilfried Bony helped himself to two goals against defensively-ragged Cherries as City remained top of the Premier League, the hosts' firepower proving too much for Eddie Howe's team.

Howe insisted Cherries would not hide behind a bumper injury crisis which worsened during the warm-up when goalkeeper Artur Boruc withdrew due to a thigh strain.

"We are going to have to cope," said Howe. "I still believe the team and the squad we have is able to be competitive, despite the fact we have so many players out long term.

"We are not looking at that as an excuse or an issue. We have to try to find a way to make them competitive. With our full squad this is an incredibly tough task but even more so with the players we have out.

"I thought we showed character in the second half, we dug in and made it more difficult. In saying that, we did cause them problems with the ball and there was a spell during the first half where I felt we were on top but we couldn't maintain it."

C4L
C4L
C4L
AIA
AIA
27
BORUC
1
PROTEK

AIA

AIA

❶ Harry Kane slots the ball past Artur Boruc
❷ Eddie Howe post match
❸ Adam Smith and Kyle Walker
❹ Eric Dier looks to close down Marc Pugh
❺ Matt Ritchie in action
❻ Charlie Daniels closes down Erik Lamela
❼ Spurs celebrate a goal

MATCHDAY 10: CHERRIES 1 TOTTENHAM 5

VITALITY STADIUM

25.10.15

A second successive 5-1 hammering – with Harry Kane plundering a hat-trick – heightened concerns Cherries could stay the course, with the manner of the defeat particularly worrying.

Although Matt Ritchie fired Cherries in front with a well-taken goal after just 49 seconds, the lead quickly evaporated when Kane netted from the spot having been brought down by Artur Boruc.

Further goals before the break from Mousa Dembélé and Erik Lamela put Spurs in control and Cherries were put out of their misery when Kane completed his treble in the second half.

Goalkeeper Boruc, restored to the starting line-up at the expense of Adam Federici, had a day to forget as he was at fault for two of the visitors' goals and also conceded the penalty.

He spilled a Kane cross at the feet of Lamela and scooped a header from Toby Alderweireld straight into the path of the England striker for him to complete his hat-trick.

Boss Eddie Howe refused to point the finger at Boruc and admitted Cherries needed to find a quick cure for their defensive frailties.

He said: "There is certainly going to be no finger-pointing or blame attached to anybody or any one individual. It's very important through success and failure that you take collective responsibility.

"We can't keep giving away goals and it has been our Achilles heel all season. Even in games we have won and drawn, we have managed to find a way to give a team a goal."

22
27
MANSION
.com

veho
MANSION
7
11

❶ Graziano Pelle scores for Saints
❷ A dejected Glenn Murray
❸ Marc Pugh in action
❹ Andrew Surman is felled
❺ Lee Tomlin and Maya Yoshida

MATCHDAY 11: SOUTHAMPTON 2 CHERRIES 0

ST MARY'S STADIUM

01.11.15

Cherries' hotly-anticipated derby with Southampton ended in disappointment as the visitors were comfortably beaten at Saint Mary's.

Eddie Howe's side were put to the sword by the dominant Saints in the opening 45 minutes, the hosts opening up a two-goal lead courtesy of Steven Davis and Graziano Pelle.

And while Cherries were much-improved following the resumption, Southampton held firm to record a 2-0 victory and subject their neighbours to a third straight Premier League defeat.

The loss soured the return to league action of Harry Arter, the midfielder making his top-flight bow having come back from injury in the League Cup reverse at Liverpool five days earlier.

And the former Woking man did not hold back in his post-match assessment, admitting he had been embarrassed by the first-half display.

Arter told the Daily Echo: "It was a poor first half. It was nowhere near good enough and at this level, we can't afford to have halves like that.

"I would say everything was missing in the first half – the whole performance wasn't good enough. We didn't keep the ball and we didn't press well. Everyone took responsibility for that and we will just have to try to improve.

"As individuals, no one likes playing the way we did in the first half. I was a little bit embarrassed by the performance.

"They were taking the mickey out of us and rightly so."

❶ Andrew Surman post match
❷ Newcastle celebrate
❸ Harry Arter in action
❹ Simon Francis applauds the supporters
❺ Charlie Daniels in action
❻ Tokelo Rantie
❼ Cherries in defensive mode
❽ Matt Ritchie after a chance goes begging

MATCHDAY 12: CHERRIES 0 NEWCASTLE 1

VITALITY STADIUM 07.11.15

Keeper Rob Elliot shrugged off thigh trouble to produce a string of fine saves as Newcastle grabbed three unlikely points at Vitality Stadium.

Ayoze Perez secured victory when he beat Adam Federici with the Magpies' only shot on target in the 27th minute, sending Cherries into the Premier League relegation zone.

The home side had enjoyed more than two-thirds of possession and 20 shots at goal but simply could not find a way through, leaving Newcastle boss Steve McClaren to brand his team's win "unexplainable".

The defeat was Cherries' eighth in their debut campaign in the top flight – as many as throughout the whole of the previous season when they won the Championship.

However, Cherries manager Eddie Howe remained upbeat.

He told the Daily Echo: "In some respects, it brings some realism to the situation. We've got a fight on our hands.

"There is no negativity from our perspective, only positivity on the back of such a dominant performance against a good side. We have to look at that aspect and take it into our next game.

"It was a tough result to take. I was very pleased with the performance, probably bar the final 15 minutes when I thought we panicked and made some bad decisions on the ball. But for the vast majority of the game, we dominated possession and chances.

"Sometimes, football does play tricks with you where you can be so dominant and still lose. We've had that before."

MATCHDAY 13: SWANSEA CITY 2 CHERRIES 2

LIBERTY STADIUM

21.11.15

Cherries surrendered a 2-0 lead but claimed a valuable point from a controversial draw with Swansea City at Liberty Stadium.

Striker Joshua King opened the scoring and his goal account for Cherries when he expertly steered home from close range after 10 minutes.

And the lead was doubled midway through the first half when Dan Gosling finished a superb team move with a precision shot into the roof of the net.

However, a cheeky back-heel by Andre Ayew reduced the deficit before Cherries stand-in skipper Simon Francis was harshly judged by referee Andre Marriner to have fouled Ayew in the box, with Jonjo Shelvey despatching the resultant penalty.

Ayew took a tumble as he vied for possession with Francis and replays showed the Ghanaian had appeared to trip himself.

Asked by the Daily Echo afterwards whether he felt referees should have to front up to the media, Francis said: "I think it would be a positive.

"You never see referees interviewed after games and questioned about their decisions.

"It is not so anyone can have a dig at them or the press can have a pop, it is just to get their view on things.

"I think it would clear up a lot of things to know what they were thinking after making the decisions. I am sure it would stop managers and players getting so angry.

"In the heat of the moment, you want to contest every decision. But if they came out and explained then it would probably make things a bit easier."

❶ Cherries celebrate Dan Gosling's strike
❷ Junior Stanislas in action
❸ Matt Ritchie evades Leon Britton

MANSION
MANSION
MANSION
MANSION
CAPTAIN
30
2
6
AFCB
KING
17
25

MATCHDAY 14: CHERRIES 3 EVERTON 3

VITALITY STADIUM

28.11.15

Dean Court witnessed one of the most sensational fightbacks in Cherries history as Junior Stanislas equalised in the eighth minute of added time.

Eddie Howe's troops had seemed destined for heartbreak when England international Ross Barkley scored against the run of play in the 95th minute.

Ramiro Funes Mori and Romelu Lukaku had handed the Toffees a two-goal lead at the interval, only for Cherries to produce a rousing comeback in the final 10 minutes.

Substitute Adam Smith's 25-yard blockbuster gave the hosts hope and a Stanislas strike seemingly secured a share of the spoils with four minutes left.

Barkley's low drive squirmed under half-time substitute Ryan Allsop, but Stanislas headed home Charlie Daniels's cross to send Dean Court into raptures.

Stunned boss Eddie Howe told the Daily Echo: "I couldn't believe it. With how our season has unfolded to this point, it felt like one of those here-we-go-again moments.

"I felt we started well until the injury to Adam Federici but the delay in the game seemed to affect us and maybe sparked Everton into life.

"From that moment until half-time, we found it difficult but in the second half we had them penned in and were doing everything but scoring.

"We really needed Adam Smith's goal to give us the belief we could get something from the game."

❶ Cherries rush towards the supporters after Junior Stanislas's late equaliser
❷ Harry Arter in action
❸ Eddie Howe and Adam Smith post match
❹ Everton after their 95th-minute strike
❺ Adam Smith after his goal

MATCHDAY 15: CHELSEA 0 CHERRIES 1

STAMFORD BRIDGE

05.12.15

Substitute Glenn Murray netted with eight minutes remaining as Cherries claimed a stunning first league win at Stamford Bridge.

Both sides had a string of chances to break the deadlock and despite plenty of second-half pressure from the Blues, it was Murray that provided the winning goal with a close-range header.

Fit-again keeper Artur Boruc, who made his first start since the end of October, kept his second clean sheet of the campaign.

Cherries climbed out of the relegation zone as of a result of victory, their first top-flight win since mid-September, while the fixture was to prove Jose Mourinho's penultimate Premier League game in charge of the Blues.

Match-winner Murray told the Daily Echo: "I felt as if I jumped on the boys' bandwagon a little bit because they worked extremely hard from the start and did the job – I just put the icing on the cake.

"No player is happy sitting on the bench, I'm not and neither are any of the lads next to me but we're paid to be ready and come on to try our best and luckily, something dropped for us.

"I think anyone gets a good feeling when you come on and score at Chelsea in the last 10 minutes and I thought we presented ourselves very well.

"It is brilliant for the lads and for the club. You could see how much it meant and, hopefully, we can kick on from here."

MANSION
MANSION

MATCHDAY 16: CHERRIES 2 MANCHESTER UTD 1

VITALITY STADIUM

12.12.15

Joshua King scored a dramatic winner against his former club to help Cherries claim another memorable Premier League victory.

King, released by Manchester United in 2013, found the net midway through the second half and later admitted the goal had "meant a lot".

The match was marked by a superb display from midfielder Harry Arter, whose world had fallen apart days earlier when fiancée Rachel had given birth to their stillborn daughter.

Junior Stanislas got Cherries off and running when his inswinging corner crept into the top corner inside the opening two minutes.

United restored parity when Marouane Fellaini poked home from close range midway through the first half.

But the final say went to King, who finished with aplomb after fastening on to Matt Ritchie's well-worked corner.

Midfielder Dan Gosling revealed afterwards how the dressing room had united in a pre-match prayer for Arter led by club chaplain Andy Rimmer.

And the former Newcastle man also said Arter had been given a standing ovation by his peers following the final whistle.

Gosling told the Daily Echo: "We had a little prayer before the game. Andy came in to do it and we were all together afterwards as well.

"After Junior's first goal, we all went over to H and it was very emotional. When he came back in, he got a standing ovation because to play in the manner he did under those circumstances was great testament to him and his family."

❶ Joshua King shows his delight after scoring against his old club
❷ King is mobbed by his team-mates
❸ Fellaini scores for United
❹ Junior Stanislas celebrates

MANSION
FRANCIS
2
DANIELS
11
6
27
tel 01202 52
web: www.cutwiseflooring

MANSION

❶ Charlie Daniels wheels away after his penalty
❷ Matt Ritchie at The Hawthorns
❸ Adam Smith in agony after James McClean's horror tackle
❹ Cherries celebrate Smith's goal

MATCHDAY 17: WEST BROM 1 CHERRIES 2

THE HAWTHORNS

19.12.15

A last-gasp penalty from Charlie Daniels secured victory at nine-man West Brom and gave Cherries a third Premier League win on the bounce.

Left-back Daniels smashed home his first goal of the season off the underside of the bar after Dan Gosling had been brought down by Baggies skipper Darren Fletcher.

James McClean had earlier been dismissed for a rash challenge on Adam Smith, moments after the Cherries defender had beaten McClean to a 50-50 ball.

Smith silenced the home supporters after the break with a terrific strike from outside the box, before Gareth McAuley equalised.

But Daniels's penalty three minutes from time ensured the visitors took home three hard-earned points, while Salomon Rondon was dismissed following an altercation with Gosling late on.

Reflecting on McClean's red-card challenge, Smith told the Daily Echo: "I thought it was a very dangerous tackle.

"I could see out of the corner of my eye that he was sprinting towards me so I knocked the ball forward and jumped because I knew he was going to come for me.

"It was lucky that I did because I think if I had stayed on the ground, my standing leg could have got hurt.

"He could have done a lot of damage because it was right in my shin and the challenge was quite hard as well.

"He lost his head at times but I don't think he did it to intentionally hurt me."

MATCHDAY 18: CHERRIES 0 CRYSTAL PALACE 0

VITALITY STADIUM 26.12.15

Cherries failed to land a knockout blow despite dominating for large spells in the 0-0 Boxing Day draw at Vitality Stadium.

The home side had the best chance to break the deadlock midway through the first half but a misunderstanding between Glenn Murray and Matt Ritchie saw both players try to convert Junior Stanislas's cross.

For Eddie Howe's side, though, a point was another step in the right direction during a successful December following wins against Chelsea, Manchester United and West Brom.

Howe, who presided over his 350th game as a manager, felt Cherries' defending of set-pieces had been the stand-out feature of the stalemate.

He told the Daily Echo: "It was a real battle. Palace are a very good side, very physical and we certainly knew we were in a game.

"The most pleasing aspect from my perspective was the way we fought and the way we defended set-plays. They are a real threat aerially and I thought we really stood up well to that test.

"That for me was the stand-out thing for us and the positive to take because Palace are very good from set-plays.

"It is not something you would associate to us as a huge strength but we dealt very well with the situations.

"We would love to have won but we were pleased. I thought we created the best chances but, unfortunately for us, we didn't take them. We spurned our best chances in the end."

❶ Charlie Daniels prepares for a throw-in
❷ Harry Arter in action
❸ The players come together over a foul on Wilfried Zaha
❹ Simon Francis and Tokelo Rantie applaud the supporters

FULL DAY OUT THAT'S GREAT, FOR YEARS 0-8!
Farmer Palmer's
FARM PARK
OPEN DAILY FROM 10AM
BUY YOUR ANNUAL PASS ONLINE
GREAT VALUE FOR MONEY, STAY AND PLAY ALL DAY!
FULL TIMETABLE OF ANIMAL HANDLING EVENTS
PONY GROOMING
PIG RACING
COW MILKING
DAILY LAMB FEEDING
MEET A GUINEA PIG
WEEKEND & HOLIDAYS PONY RIDES *
TRACTOR RIDES
WOODLAND WALK
INDOOR PLAY AND OUTDOOR WHATEVER THE WEATHER
* Extra charge for Pony rides
CERTIFICATE of EXCELLENCE 2015 Winner
tripadvisor
2015 AWARD WINNERS
YOUR FAMILY FRIENDLY FARM PARK!
call. 01202 622022
email. shop@farmerpalmers.co.uk
www.farmerpalmers.co.uk
Wareham Road, Organford, Poole, BH16 6EU
Find us on
APPROVED family friendly ATTRACTION 2016/17 GOLD
approvedfamilyfriendly.com
DORSET
Tourism Awards 2015
SILVER

1 - 7 Charminster Road
Charminster, Dorset
BH8 8UE
01202 311 514
bournemouth@creamscafe.com
CREAMS BOURNEMOUTH
CreamsCafeBournemouth
Creams Bournemouth
creamsbournemouth
creamsBMouth
Creams
THE ITALIAN GELATO & DE
GELATO Co
ELATO C
OPENING TIMES
SUN-THUR 10AM TO 11PM
FRI-SAT 10AM TO MIDNIGHT
WAFFLES • CREPES • SUNDAES • MILKSHAKES • CATER BIRTHDAY PARTIES

CHAMBERLAIN
15
30
3

❶ Mesut Ozil celebrates his goal at the Emirates
❷ Harry Arter in action
❸ Steve Cook chests down
❹ Matt Ritchie keeps his eyes on Aaron Ramsey
❺ Joshua King in action

MATCHDAY 19: ARSENAL 2 CHERRIES 0

EMIRATES STADIUM

28.12.15

Cherries' six-match unbeaten streak was brought to a grinding halt as World Cup-winner Mesut Ozil pulled the strings at Emirates Stadium.

The German international supplied an assist for Gabriel when his inswinging corner was firmly diverted into the top corner by the Brazilian, who had cleverly located space in a packed penalty area.

And just after the hour mark, Ozil played a sublime one-two with striker Olivier Giroud and slotted through the legs of stopper Artur Boruc.

Cherries battled gamely and enjoyed moments of their own but, ultimately, it was a relatively comfortable victory for Arsene Wenger's side in the first league encounter between the teams.

Visiting boss Eddie Howe admitted to mixed feelings over his team's display, telling the Daily Echo: "It was really disappointing because I thought we were very good in the early stages of the game, gave a really good account of ourselves and played our way.

"I thought we had them on the back foot at times but then we conceded the first goal. We just seemed to lose our way totally until the break.

"I would say that's very unusual for us and the manner of the goal didn't help. Set-pieces then became a problem and it took us until half-time to recover.

"The second half took a similar pattern where we were in control but couldn't break down a stubborn defence."

MATCHDAY 28: CHERRIES 2 SOUTHAMPTON 0

VITALITY STADIUM

01.03.16

In light of a battling away performance, the spotlight turned on Cherries having the second-worst home record in the Premier League.

That was soon banished to the memory banks, though, as Eddie Howe's men created another little piece of history in emphatic style.

Steve Cook's stunner and a poacher's finish from Benik Afobe secured a first league victory over Southampton in 58 years in a cauldron of noise at Vitality Stadium.

Lacklustre Saints were second best in every battle admitted irate boss Ronald Koeman afterwards as Cherries stretched to eight points their lead over the relegation places.

Koeman said: "It was not good enough.

"There was also a big difference with how they started the game, how they were hungry and winning challenges that we didn't and that was from second one.

"That was not tactics, that was belief, spirit, character, mentality."

Howe purred: "We spoke in the build-up about the importance of the game to them because it had been a long time since we had beaten Southampton and there was local rivalry at stake.

"It was a massive result as well for our survival hopes.

"On the back of the Watford game, we wanted to build on that and we did."

The match also saw fourth official Kevin Friend sent to hospital after collapsing and hitting his head on the Southampton dugout.

He was replaced at half-time by a referee who happened to be in the crowd, Dean Treleaven.

KING
17
PUGH
7

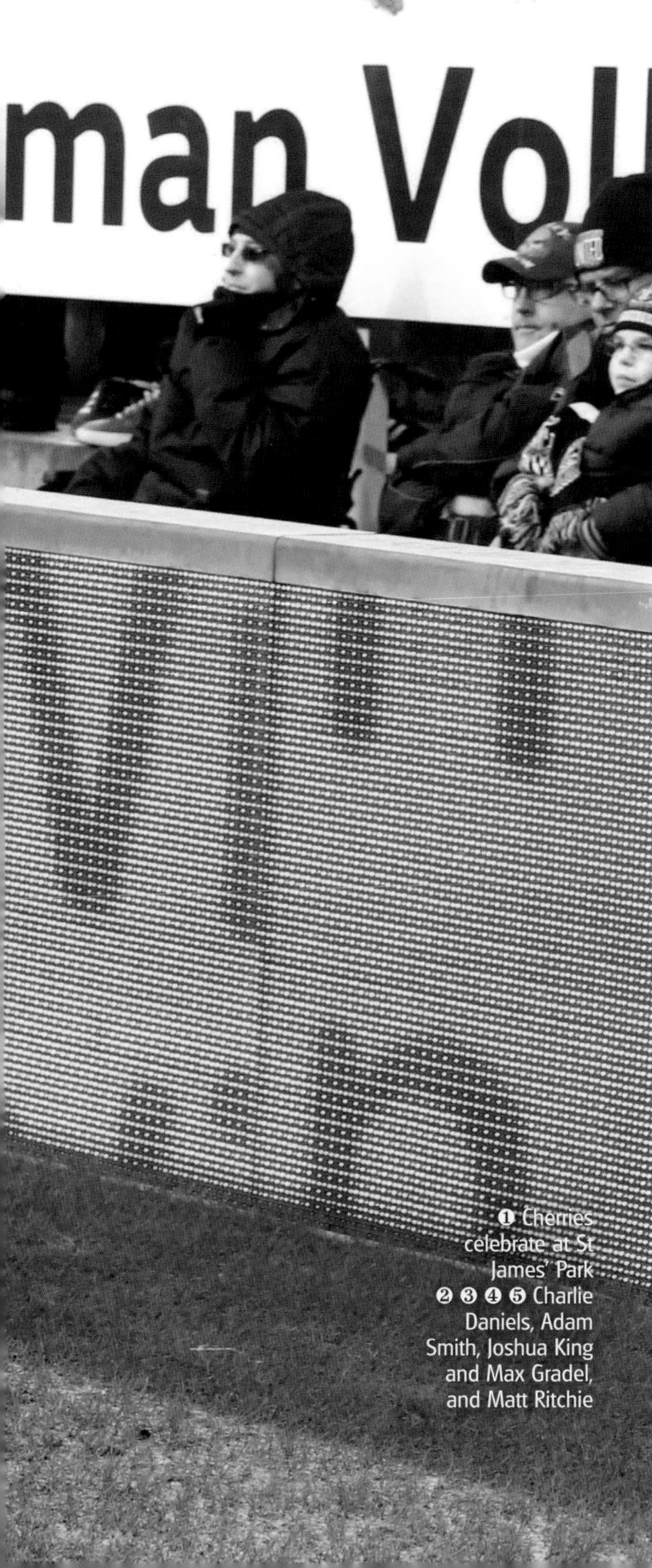

❶ Cherries celebrate at St James' Park ❷ ❸ ❹ ❺ Charlie Daniels, Adam Smith, Joshua King and Max Gradel, and Matt Ritchie

MATCHDAY 29: NEWCASTLE 1 CHERRIES 3

ST JAMES' PARK

05.03.16

Every inch of the 696-mile round trip – the longest in the Premier League – was made worthwhile on a surreal afternoon on Tyneside.

The knives were out for home boss Steve McClaren on the back of poor form and a bust up with a journalist and Cherries made the most of the toxic atmosphere at St James' Park.

The visitors earned a slice of luck when Joshua King, irrepressible all afternoon, saw his cross from the left deflected into this own net by Steven Taylor.

The boos rang out at half-time but Newcastle's insipid display continued and King doubled the lead by rifling beyond Rob Elliot.

Ayoze Perez gave the Magpies hope but a rapier move down the left ended with Charlie Daniels coolly slotting home a decisive third in stoppage time.

McClaren was forced to bat away a series of probing questions about his future but was sacked and replaced by Rafael Benitez six days later.

A beaming Eddie Howe had only one concern – trying to play down the notion that Cherries had secured safety through the result.

"No, it is not us 'just about there'. We have a lot more work to do," said Howe in his post-match address.

"We play Swansea next week, the games get bigger from our perspective.

"We don't want to let up until we know we're safe and even if we are to hit that mark, then we want even more."

T: 01202 538800
GRADEL
10

❶ Steve Cook celebrates his goal with Lewis Grabban
❷ Eddie Howe and Jason Tindall post-match
❸ Joshua King is mobbed
❹ Max Gradel embraces Eddie Howe

MATCHDAY 30: CHERRIES 3 SWANSEA CITY 2

VITALITY STADIUM

12.03.16

They think it's all over... Okay, Cherries had not quite finished the job but victory in a match billed as a last dash for the safety line made it difficult for Eddie Howe to deny it was mission accomplished.

In truth, Cherries were not at their best but were belligerent in an open, entertaining game between two teams renowned for their bright, passing philosophies.

Max Gradel bagged his first Premier League goal in the red and black some eight years after his last Cherries goals, a brace at home to Millwall in League One while on loan from Leicester.

The home side's patient probing had paid off but not for long as a momentary lapse allowed persistent menace Mo Barrow to cut in and find the far corner within two minutes.

Joshua King lashed home off the neat post, ruthlessly exploiting another Lukasz Fabianski aberration five minutes after the interval but more ponderous defending saw Gylfi Sigurdsson's swerving finish from Barrow's cutback level matters for a second time.

Cherries wobbled at 2-2 with burly Swansea substitute Bafetimbi Gomis wreaking havoc up front.

However, having regained control of the ball, Matt Ritchie delivered a delicious cross that was crying out to be converted by Steve Cook.

The match-winner said: "There was a quote today – who slows down when you can see the finish line?

"We want to finish as high as possible. We are proud of what we have done so far but everyone is very ambitious.

"There is no reason to stop. We've got some great games coming but there is a little less pressure now."

❶ Dejected Cherries after a Spurs goal
❷ Toby Alderweireld keeps tabs on Matt Ritchie
❸ Adam Smith after Harry Kane scores
❹ Joshua King in action at White Hart Lane
❺ Steve Cook and Charlie Daniels

MATCHDAY 31: TOTTENHAM 3 CHERRIES 0

WHITE HART LANE

20.03.16

Cherries were again put to the sword by England star Harry Kane as their first trip to White Hart Lane ended in an emphatic 3-0 defeat.

Striker Kane, who bagged a hat-trick in the teams' only previous league meeting in October, was again in ruthless mood as he registered twice in the opening 16 minutes.

A Christian Eriksen tap-in soon after the restart ensured beyond reasonable doubt that there was no way back for Cherries.

Visiting boss Eddie Howe admitted there had been plenty to admire about the display of Mauricio Pochettino's side.

Howe said: "In the two games they have been excellent against us. I don't think it has helped that we have not hit our levels in either game but there is a lot we can take from them.

"They make the pitch very big and stretch you. You want to have the ball and they make it very difficult for you to get it with their tactical play, especially deep in their own half. They have players who are comfortable with the ball.

"From both sides, they switched the play very well and stretched our midfield and back four. Then you have the quality of Harry Kane in the front position. When he gets time, he hurts you.

"They work very hard but have a lot of good quality on the ball as well and we would aspire to be them one day."

NFERENCE OR EVEN AT A

MANGALA
20

MATCHDAY 32:
CHERRIES 0 MANCHESTER CITY 4
VITALITY STADIUM
02.04.16

❶ Manchester City celebrate Kevin de Bruyne's goal
❷ Lewis Grabban tussles with Fernandinho
❸ Grabban in action
❹ Cherries shake hands post match

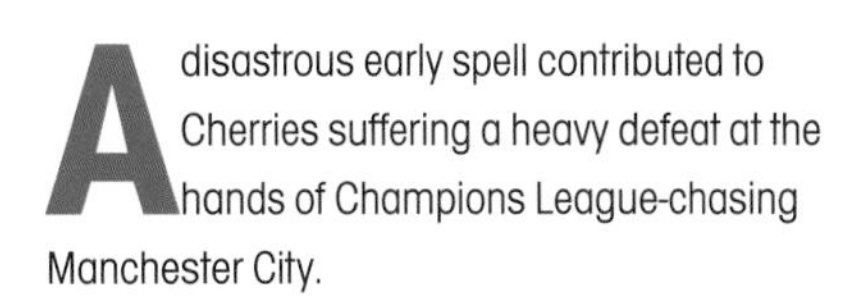

A disastrous early spell contributed to Cherries suffering a heavy defeat at the hands of Champions League-chasing Manchester City.

Eddie Howe's team conceded three times in the space of 12 minutes as the visitors made a flying start at Vitality Stadium.

Fernando got the ball rolling when he clipped home a delightful opener after Cherries had failed to deal with Jesus Navas's seventh-minute corner.

De Bruyne then marked his first appearance for two months with a finely-taken second, the Belgian volleying past Artur Boruc in the 12th minute.

And City's leading goalscorer Sergio Aguero left Cherries with a mountain to climb when he headed home number three after 19 minutes.

Aleksandar Kolarov came off the bench to rifle home a fourth goal in second-half stoppage time.

Cherries striker Lewis Grabban, who made his first top-flight start since re-signing from Norwich in January, revealed his disappointment at the result.

Grabban said: "Personally, getting a start didn't matter, the result took away any good feeling I had. Getting beaten 4-0 was not nice for any of us and was the only thing on my mind.

"Afterwards it was a mixture of everything – disappointment and anger with ourselves at the way we lost and the mistakes we made.

"We want to finish the season as positively as possible and that was not good enough from us.

"They got three goals in quick succession and that was probably when we were in shock. But we knew their threats and that we had put them in their stride with the first goal."

MATCHDAY 33: ASTON VILLA 1 CHERRIES 2

VILLA PARK
09.04.16

Quality goals from Steve Cook and Joshua King saw Cherries all but secure their Premier League status and effectively seal Aston Villa's relegation to the Championship.

Victory in the Midlands saw Eddie Howe's team move to 41 points – 14 clear of Sunderland who occupied the final relegation berth.

Cook's stunning opener on the stroke of half-time paved the way for victory before King's majestic finish made it 2-0 with 16 minutes remaining.

And although Villa managed to halve the deficit through Jordan Ayew five minutes from time, Cherries held out comfortably.

Callum Wilson finally put an end to his lengthy injury nightmare when he came off the bench late on, while skipper Tommy Elphick made his first league start since September.

Boss Howe reiterated his commitment to Cherries after the final whistle and insisted there would be no let-up in his bid to continue to take the club forward.

Asked about the possibility of bigger clubs looking at him in light of his success with Cherries, Howe said: "I am absolutely committed to the challenges I face here and am committed to AFC Bournemouth as much as I ever have been.

"I want to take this club into new ground all the time.

"I think that is the beauty of this club. We had never been here before so you are constantly trying to make history and trying to leave a legacy. I still feel there is a lot more work to do."

❶ Callum Wilson during his comeback game
❷ Cherries celebrate
❸ Joshua King in action
❹ More celebrations for Howe's side
❺ Shaun MacDonald keeps his eyes on the ball

❶ Tommy Elphick and Lucas Leiva lay a wreath in memory of the Hillsborough disaster victims
❷ Matt Ritchie battles with Reds captain Lucas
❸ Liverpool celebrate Daniel Sturridge's goal
❹ Jurgen Klopp before the game

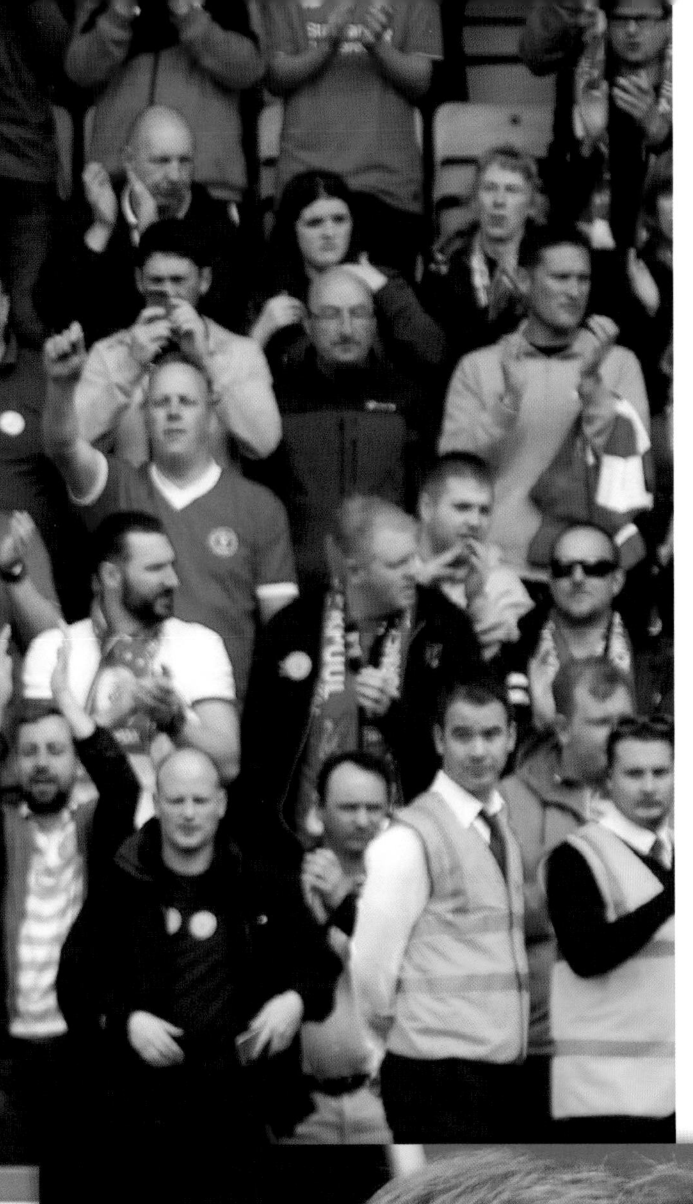

MATCHDAY 34: CHERRIES 1 LIVERPOOOL 2

VITALITY STADIUM

16.04.16

Goals from Roberto Firmino and Daniel Sturridge delayed the party at Vitality Stadium as Cherries were forced to wait to celebrate staying in the Premier League.

Victory over a much-changed Liverpool team would have ensured Cherries' top-flight status but it all went to pot towards the end of the first half when the visitors netted twice.

Firmino tapped home from inside the six-yard box to open the scoring after 41 minutes before Sturridge doubled the lead in first-half stoppage time.

The quick-fire double left Eddie Howe's team with a mountain to climb in the second period and, although Joshua King halved the deficit in added time, they were unable to find a late leveller.

Midfielder Andrew Surman admitted Cherries had not stayed in the game long enough to make a home win a realistic aim.

He said: "We probably didn't play as well as we have done and didn't give ourselves the best chance.

"There were not enough players at it.

"Having said that, we were still level after 40 minutes and if we could have got to half-time at 0-0, I think it could have been a completely different second half.

"Unfortunately, as was the case in three recent games against top sides, we were out of the game at half-time.

"When you are chasing games against teams like Liverpool, Manchester City and Spurs, it's very difficult to get back into it and you leave yourself open to conceding more goals."

SINGHA

❶ Steve Cook looks on as Willian scores for Chelsea
❷ Chelsea celebrate Eden Hazard's goal
❸ Simon Francis battles with Diego Costa
❹ Tommy Elphick celebrates his goal
❺ Guus Hiddink and Eddie Howe

MATCHDAY 35: CHERRIES 1 CHELSEA 4

VITALITY STADIUM

23.04.16

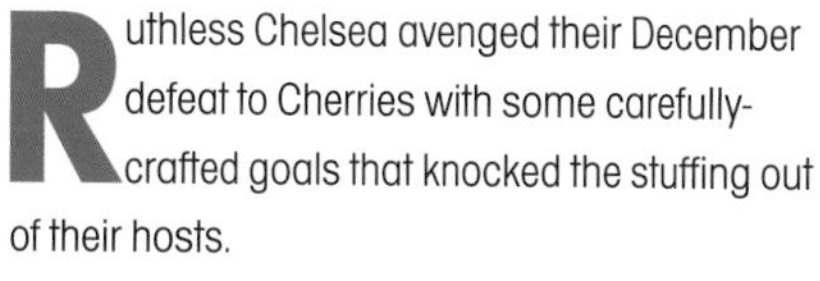

Ruthless Chelsea avenged their December defeat to Cherries with some carefully-crafted goals that knocked the stuffing out of their hosts.

Like so many matches in their tricky end-of-season run, Cherries started brightly but paid the price for gifting Chelsea's stars – Cesc Fabregas in particular – too much room.

The Spain international released winger Pedro to clip past Artur Boruc early on and then created Eden Hazard's strike with a cheeky backheel 11 minutes before the break.

Tommy Elphick guided home moments later, handing Cherries a lifeline their purposeful attacking play had deserved and prompted a flurry of second-half pressure.

Junior Stanislas bent an effort narrowly wide of the upright, while the introduction of substitutes Callum Wilson and Benik Afobe briefly gave Cherries fresh impetus.

But when Fabregas picked out Willian to drive home Chelsea's third on the break, the game was up with Hazard adding gloss to the scoreline in injury time.

"I thought it was a really even game, especially in the first half where I thought we were terrific," said boss Eddie Howe.

"The difference between the teams was how they finished their goals. We created enough chances in the first half but didn't have that clinical edge that they did.

"We went near enough up against their best side and caused them problems. You have to admire their quality."

MATCHDAY 36: EVERTON 2 CHERRIES 1

GOODISON PARK

30.04.16

Cherries ultimately guaranteed their Premier League status for next season despite defeat in a keenly-contested match at Everton.

The under-fire hosts, whose boss Roberto Martinez was the subject of fans' protests throughout, got off to the perfect start when England international Ross Barkley teed up Tom Cleverley to net a sumptuous opener.

Cleverley picked up possession and following some mesmerising movement on the edge of the penalty area, thumped low across Artur Boruc.

Cherries hit straight back with Callum Wilson, making his first start since suffering anterior cruciate ligament damage at Stoke in September, brushing aside Everton youngster Matthew Pennington to find Marc Pugh to force home his third top-flight goal.

The home side took advantage of some second-half pressure with that man Barkley again at the hub of a move which ended with left-back Leighton Baines finding the roof of the net from Aaron Lennon's low centre.

Cherries continued to create openings with Benik Afobe guilty of spurning the best opportunity in what was a marked improvement on recent performances from Eddie Howe's men.

The Cherries manager said: "I thought it was an even game and a good battle between two decent teams.

"How we conceded two goals was a difficult one to work out from our perspective because I thought we looked solid defensively."

❶ Callum Wilson shows his frustration
❷ Harry Arter in action
❸ Everton celebrate
❹ Marc Pugh and team-mates after the winger's strike

❶ The Cherries squad on a lap of honour following the final home game of the campaign
❷ Chairman Jeff Mostyn post-match
❸ Matt Ritchie wheels away after his goal
❹ Steve Cook plays out from the back
❺ Junior Stanislas in action

MATCHDAY 37: CHERRIES 1 WEST BROM 1

VITALITY STADIUM

07.05.16

Substitute Matt Ritchie headed a late equaliser as Cherries snatched a point in their final home game of the season.

But it was the heroics of goalkeeper Artur Boruc that proved critical as the Polish international atoned for his role in West Brom's opener.

The stopper's poor clearance resulted in Jonathan Leko finding Jonny Evans, whose left-wing cross was headed home by Salomon Rondon.

Boruc swiftly made up for the error by diverting Craig Gardner's penalty against the bar, moments later clawing off the line after Steve Cook had toe-poked the ball against Gardner.

The introduction of Callum Wilson and Joshua King in the second half breathed new life into Cherries, while Ritchie came off the bench to head home eight minutes from time.

The Scotland international capitalised after Cook's long throw had been inadvertently helped on by Claudio Yacob.

Cherries boss Eddie Howe felt Boruc's double save had been a crucial factor in the clash.

The boss said: "It was an outstanding save. Artur is an outstanding goalkeeper and he has saved some good penalties for us over the years.

"It was a massive moment for us because if we had gone down 2-0, it might have been a bridge too far.

"Before the season started, we would have bitten off arms, legs or whatever was available to be in the position we are now."

After the game, Cherries players and staff came onto the pitch to applaud the fans.

MATCHDAY 38: MANCHESTER UTD 3 CHERRIES 1

OLD TRAFFORD
17.05.16

Cherries finished their season on a low note – and 48 hours after the rest of the Premier League brought down the curtain on the 2015-16 campaign.

A bomb scare, later confirmed as a device that had been left behind following a training exercise, saw around 70,000 supporters evacuated from Old Trafford on Sunday, May 15 before the game was called off on police advice.

A hardy bunch of around 1,000 supporters made their way back up the M6 for the rearranged fixture the following Tuesday evening but were treated to a pretty dire display as United ran out comfortable winners.

In a wretched first half, Wayne Rooney's opener just before half-time was nothing less than United had deserved.

Young striker Marcus Rashford made it 2-0 midway through the second half, during which Cherries were much better, before substitute Ashley Young bagged United's third three minutes from time.

In a strange game, played out in a half empty stadium, there was still time for a Chris Smalling own goal to at least make the scoreline respectable.

Defender Simon Francis said: "We didn't play well enough.

"That was the disappointing thing for us because we were desperate to finish this season on a high.

"Manchester United made the pitch big, which they always do at home, and they can hurt you in those wide areas. Some of their goals were top class and we couldn't deal with it."

❶ A dejected Simon Francis after Wayne Rooney's opener
❷ Captain Tommy Elphick
❸ Matt Ritchie chases down Michael Carrick
❹ Elphick and Steve Cook keep their eyes on Cameron Borthwick-Jackson
❺ Callum Wilson battles with Carrick

MANSION
WILSON
13

Final table

	P	W	D	L	F	A	Pts
Leicester	38	23	12	3	68	36	81
Arsenal	38	20	11	7	65	36	71
Tottenham	38	19	13	6	69	35	70
Man City	38	19	9	10	71	41	66
Man Utd	38	19	9	10	49	35	66
Southampton	38	18	9	11	59	41	63
West Ham	38	16	14	8	65	51	62
Liverpool	38	16	12	10	63	50	60
Stoke	38	14	9	15	41	55	51
Chelsea	38	12	14	12	59	53	50
Everton	38	11	14	13	59	55	47
Swansea	38	12	11	15	42	52	47
Watford	38	12	9	17	40	50	45
West Brom	38	10	13	15	34	48	43
Crystal Palace	38	11	9	18	39	51	42
CHERRIES	38	11	9	18	45	69	42
Sunderland	38	9	12	17	48	62	39
Newcastle	38	9	10	19	44	65	37
Norwich	38	9	7	22	39	67	34
Aston Villa	38	3	8	27	27	76	17

Leading scorers

	Total	League	Cup
Joshua King	7	6	1
Marc Pugh	5	3	2
Junior Stanislas	5	3	2
Callum Wilson	5	5	0
Steve Cook	4	4	0
Dan Gosling	4	3	1
Glenn Murray	4	3	1
Benik Afobe	4	4	0
Matt Ritchie	4	4	0
Charlie Daniels	3	3	0
Adam Smith	2	2	0
Harry Arter	1	1	0
Shaun MacDonald	1	0	1
Tommy Elphick	1	1	0
Max Gradel	1	1	0

Cup results

FA Cup third round: Birmingham 1 Cherries 2 (Tomlin, Murray)

FA Cup fourth round: Portsmouth 1 Cherries 2 (King, Pugh)

FA Cup fifth round: Cherries 0 Everton 2

League Cup second round: Hartlepool 0 Cherries 4 (Kermorgant, Gosling, Stanislas, 2)

League Cup third round: Preston 2 Cherries 2 (MacDonald, Pugh) AFCB won 3-2 on penalties

League Cup fourth round: Liverpool 1 Cherries 0

This publication is dedicated to the memory of life-long AFC Bournemouth fan and photographer Mick Cunningham, who tragically died while covering the Premier League game at Stoke City for the Daily Echo.

The squad

1: Artur Boruc
2: Simon Francis
3: Steve Cook
4: Dan Gosling
5: Tommy Elphick
6: Andrew Surman
7: Marc Pugh
8: Harry Arter
9: Tokelo Rantie
10: Max Gradel
11: Charlie Daniels
12: Juan Iturbe
13: Callum Wilson
14: Tyrone Mings
15: Adam Smith
16: Shaun MacDonald
17: Joshua King
19: Junior Stanislas
20: Benik Afobe
22: Marius Adamonis
23: Adam Federici
25: Sylvain Distin
27: Glenn Murray
28: Lewis Grabban
29: Rhoys Wiggins
30: Matt Ritchie
32: Eunan O'Kane